SNOWY RIVER RIDERS

Selected Poems by A. B. Paterson   *Paintings by Robert Lovett*

SNOWY RIVER RIDERS

Selected Poems by A. B. Paterson   *Paintings by Robert Lovett*

ANGUS
& ROBERTSON

An imprint of HarperCollins*Publishers*

Details of Paintings

Watercolour : 'Mountain man', p. 14, 73cm x 50cm; 'We take the stock away', pp. 50-1, 51cm x 71cm; 'The old man', p. 64, 35cm x 46cm
Oil on canvas : 'At the melting of the snow', pp. 6-7, 61cm x 76cm; 'Wollondibby Creek, Jindabyne', pp. 8-9, 61cm x 76cm; 'Moombah Horsemen', p. 10, 40cm x 50cm; 'Red Gums of the Monaro', p. 13, 61cm x 91cm; 'The colt from Old Regret', p. 16, 41cm x 51cm; 'All the cracks had gathered to the fray', p. 17, 61cm x 91cm; 'The stripling', p. 18, 45cm x 60cm; 'He waited sad and wistful', p. 19, 46cm x 61cm; 'There was movement at the station', pp. 20-1, 46cm x 122cm; 'He hails from Snowy River', p. 22, 46cm x 60cm; 'Towards the mountain's brow', p. 23, 61cm x 91cm; 'Snowy River Riders', pp. 24-5, 46cm x 122cm; 'Then fast the horsemen followed', pp. 26-7, 38cm x 76cm; 'He was racing on the wing', pp. 28-9, 91cm x 1.8m; 'Upward ever.upward', p. 31, 91cm x 122cm; 'He raced him down the mountain', p. 32, 137cm x 122cm; 'He sent the flintstones flying', p. 33, 66cm x 61cm; 'His courage fiery hot', pp. 34-5, 46cm x 122cm; 'He was right among the horses', pp. 36-7, 51cm x 71cm;

'Turned their heads for home', pp. 38-9, 61cm x 122cm; 'The Man from Snowy River', p. 40, 107cm x 150cm; 'Murrumbidgee Country', pp. 42-3, 61cm x 91cm; 'Breaking the Ice', pp. 44-5, 61cm x 91cm; 'A Mountain Station', p. 46, 61cm x 91cm; 'We muster up with weary hearts', pp. 48-9, 61cm x 91cm; 'The mountain wind is blowing', pp. 52-3, 61cm x 91cm; 'Through the sweet green grasses springing', pp. 54-5, 41cm x 61cm; 'Leisurely the cattle pass', pp. 56-7, 61cm x 91cm; 'The cattle splash across the ford', p. 58, 46cm x 61cm; 'The old bush homestead', pp. 60-1, 46cm x 61cm; 'Kiley's Run', pp. 62-3, 61cm x 91cm; 'Brumby's Run', p. 66, 61cm x 91cm; 'The gully-rakers go', p. 67, 91cm x 107cm; 'Dim shadows on the grass', pp. 68-9, 91cm x 122cm; 'The traveller by the mountain track', p. 70, 61cm x 91cm; 'The brumby horses turn and fly', p. 71, 107cm x 150cm; 'Towards the hills again', p. 72, 61cm x 91cm; 'A rush of horses through trees', p. 73, 61cm x 91cm; 'The brumby mob go by', pp. 74-5, 91cm x 1.8m; 'Off to scour the mountainside', pp. 76-7, 61cm x 91cm; 'To ride once more on brumby's run', p. 78, 91cm x 107cm.

AN ANGUS & ROBERTSON BOOK
An imprint of HarperCollinsPublishers

First published in Australia in 1991 by
CollinsAngus&Robertson Publishers Pty Limited (ACN 009 913 517)
A division of HarperCollinsPublishers (Australia) Pty Limited
4 Eden Park, 31 Waterloo Road, North Ryde, NSW 2113, Australia

William Collins Publishers Ltd
31 View Road, Glenfield, Auckland 10, New Zealand

HarperCollinsPublishers Limited
77-85 Fulham Palace Road, London W6 8JB, United Kingdom

Copyright c Retusa Pty Ltd

Illustrations © Robert Lovett 1991

National Library of Australia
Cataloguing-in-Publication data:

Paterson, A. B. (Andrew Barton), 1864-1941.
   Snowy River riders.
   ISBN 0 207 17289 7.
   I. Lovett, Robert, 1930-   . II. Title.
A821.2

Cover illustration by Robert Lovett
Typeset in 11/16 pt New Baskerville
Printed in Hong Kong

5 4 3 2 1
95 94 93 92 91

CONTENTS

A. B. PATERSON

Andrew Barton 'Banjo' Paterson was born in 1864, the son of a station owner. Although he was actually born near Orange, he spent his childhood years at Illalong Station near Yass, New South Wales.

Illalong Station itself was situated on the main route between Sydney and Melbourne and the constant traffic of horsemen, bullock teams, drovers and coaches gave the young Barty plenty of opportunity to observe the harsh life of the bush pioneers. He also learnt of the bush experience first hand through his grandmother, a pioneer in the outback of the 1840s and 1850s.

Horses and riding were to play a major part in Paterson's life from the very beginning. Until the age of 11, he rode bareback the four miles to school everyday; and his famous pseudonym, 'Banjo', came from the name of a horse at the property.

Paterson began his adult life as a solicitor in Sydney although outdoor life remained very important to him. He was well-respected as one of Australia's best amateur riders and even won a steeplechase at Randwick as an amateur rider in 1895. He also rode hounds with the Sydney Hunt Club and was a talented polo player.

Under the encouragement of the editor of the *Bulletin*, J. F. Archibald, Paterson began writing verse about the bush and its people. 'Old pardon, the Son of Reprieve' was published in the *Bulletin* in 1888 and by the 1890s Banjo Paterson's ballads were a popular and regular feature of the magazine. In 1895,

Angus & Robertson published the first collection of his poems, *The Man from Snowy River and Other Verses* which became an immediate best-seller, selling in the thousands in its first few weeks.

In addition to his success as a writer, Paterson also pursued a successful career in journalism, reporting on the Boer War in 1899 in South Africa for the *Sydney Morning Herald* and acting as editor on two prominent Sydney newspapers.

The call of the bush remained a constant factor in Paterson's life. In 1908 he gave up his successful career in Sydney and with his wife and two children took over a property at Wee Jasper on the fringe of the Snowy River country. He also took over a wheat farm at Grenfell for a short time before returning to Sydney in 1912.

Paterson also served with distinction in World War I being appointed AIF Lieutenant in the first Australian Remount Unit where he had charge of the training and management of army horses. Of his squadron of rough riders, jackeroos, horse-breakers, ex-jockeys and buck-jumping riders from country shows, Banjo Paterson wrote they were 'the best lot of men that were ever got together to deal with rough horses'.

Into his old age Paterson continued to pursue the themes that he had loved since childhood: horses, the sporting life and writing. In 1939 he was awarded the CBE for his services to Australian literature. He died in 1941 at the age of seventy-six.

INTRODUCTION

I'll always remember that November morning in 1950. It was my twentieth birthday. After travelling all night long on the train (Old Smokey) from Sydney, I arrived in Cooma to take up my new job as artist with the Snowy Mountains Authority. I was tired. It was bleak and very cold. Cooma looked forbidding and inhospitable. I resolved there and then not to stay too long and get out of this godforsaken place as soon as possible. It was eighteen years later that I finally bid the Snowy goodbye, but part of me stayed and keeps drawing me back.

One of my first tasks was to become familiar with the hundreds of square kilometres of wild bush country in order to complete the many illustrations required for publicity. So I set off with a four wheel drive into some of the remote parts of the mountains. There were few roads. Accommodation was very basic, tents in most of the camps. I visited road construction sites and survey camps further remote. We rode horseback into the Tumut Ravine. I marvelled at the rugged beauty as the mountains revealed themselves to me.

The words of Banjo Paterson kept running through my mind:

'He hails from Snowy River, up by Kosciusko's side,
Where the hills are twice as steep and twice as rough'.

I'd learnt the poem at school, but now it took on a whole new meaning.

We rode slowly down the mountainside, so steep the horses could barely keep their feet. Over fallen logs and granite rocks, through alpine ash and mountain gum, through dense melaleuca scrub we rode to finally arrive at the river. I'd never known such unspoilt beauty, such solitude. The crystal clear water rushing over the round stones, tumbling down small waterfalls and exploding into foaming white rapids as it careered between the rock walls of the ravine.

I stood and contemplated for a long time while the horses were drinking. I felt some pangs of guilt that I was a participant in the destruction that was to come with the building of roads, dams and power stations. Oh well, that's progress! In those days technology was God.

So began my affinity with Banjo Paterson and my love of the high country. During those wonderful eighteen years I explored and painted throughout the Snowy Mountains, the Monaro and the Murray Valley. I met many wonderful characters, the people of the mountains, descendants of the original settlers. Hardy men who had made their lives in the harsh environment and impossible conditions — great horsemen and colourful characters. All this time the poem was there in the back of my mind. I thought it would make a great theme for a series of paintings. The opportunity was to present itself years later.

Meantime I purchased 800 hectares 48 kilometres east of Cooma. A cattle property sitting on the edge of the Great Dividing Range it took in 3 kilometres of the Badja River. Tall timber clad hills dipped down to the cleared country along the river. A small cottage nestled amongst the snow gums on a knoll overlooking the river. Almost all weekends were spent with my wife and three sons at Badja Springs, as we named it.

It was a mixture of work and play. We ran about 300 cattle but found the time for horseriding and trout fishing. I painted the landscape, the cattle and the horses. I was seduced by the natural beauty of the bush that surrounded us. The practical considerations of raising cattle came a poor second to the impulse to paint.

Again the Banjo Paterson images were all around me. We had flood and drought and bushfire. We rode in blizzards rounding up cattle. We lost cattle, we fed cattle, we sent cattle away on agistment. There were highs as well, like when the cattle grew fat on good pasture and we topped the yearling market.

It was 1981 when I heard of the production of the movie 'The Man from Snowy River'. I decided it was time to do the paintings. I had made contact with the movie producer, Geoff Burrows, who made me welcome and invited me on location for the filming in Victoria. This provided the inspiration I needed, but in the main I drew from my experience in the Snowy Mountains for most of the settings. The final

collection formed an exhibition in the Sydney Opera House, coinciding with the release of the movie.

On opening night the Opera House gallery was packed with people including the movie stars and production people. Jack Thompson recited the poem to a hushed audience and brought a tear to many an eye.

This collection of poems forms word pictures that I can identify with. Each one describes the places, the characters and events of my own experience. Banjo Paterson's verse takes me back even further to my early childhood in a bark hut on the banks of the Barrington River. But that's another story. The art of writing and the art of painting are much akin and seem to require the same involvement and mental process.

A great admiration for the work of Banjo Paterson and a love of the mountains and mountain people have inspired, I hope, a worthy collection of visual images to support the magnificent poetry of the *Snowy River Riders*.

ROBERT LOVETT

◆ At the Melting of the Snow ◆

There's a sunny southern land,
   And it's there that I would be
Where the big hills stand,
   In the south countrie!
When the wattles bloom again,
   Then it's time for us to go
To the old Monaro country
   At the melting of the snow.

To the east or to the west,
  Or wherever you may be,
You will find no place
  Like the south countrie.
For the skies are blue above,
  And the grass is green below,
In the old Monaro country
  At the melting of the snow.

✤ A T T H E M E L T I N G O F T H E S N O W ✤

Now the team is in the plough,
  And the thrushes start to sing,
And the pigeons on the bough
  Are rejoicing at the spring.
So come my comrades all,
  Let us saddle up and go
To the old Monaro country
  At the melting of the snow.

◆ THE MOUNTAIN SQUATTER ◆

Here in my mountain home,
  On rugged hills and steep,
I sit and watch you come,
  Oh Riverina Sheep!

You come from fertile plains
  Where saltbush (sometimes) grows,
And flats that (when it rains)
  Will blossom like the rose.

But when the summer sun
  Gleams down like burnished brass
You have to leave your run
  And hustle off for grass.

'Tis then that — forced to roam —
  You come to where I keep,
Here in my mountain home,
  A boarding-house for sheep.

Around me where I sit
  The wary wombat goes,
A beast of little wit
  But what he knows, he *knows*.

The very same remark
  Applies to me also,
I don't give out a spark,
  But what I know, I *know*.

My brain perhaps would show
  No convolutions deep;
But anyhow I know
  The way to handle sheep.

These Riverina cracks,
  They do not care to ride
The half-inch hanging tracks
  Along the mountain side.

Their horses shake with fear
  When loosened boulders go,
With leaps, like startled deer,
  Down to the gulfs below.

Their very dogs will shirk,
  And drop their tails in fright
When asked to go and work
  A mob that's out of sight.

My little collie pup
  Works silently and wide,
You'll see her climbing up
  Along the mountain side.

As silent as a fox
  You'll see her come and go
A shadow through the rocks
  Where ash and messmate grow.

Then, lost to sight and sound
  Behind some rugged steep,
She works her way around
  And gathers up the sheep.

And working wide and shy,
  She holds them rounded up.
The cash ain't coined to buy
  That little collie pup.

And so I draw a screw
  For self and dog and keep
To boundary ride for you,
  Oh Riverina Sheep!

And when the autumn rain
  Has made the herbage grow,
You travel off again,
  And glad — no doubt — to go!

But some are left behind
  Around the mountain's spread,
For those we cannot find
  We put them down as dead.

But when we say *adieu*
  And close the boarding job,
I always find a few
  Fresh earmarks in my mob.

So what with those I sell,
  And what with those I keep,
You pay me pretty well,
  Oh Riverina Sheep!

✤ T H E M O U N T A I N S Q U A T T E R ✤

It's up to me to shout
  Before we say goodbye —
"Here's to a howlin' drought
  All west of Gundagai!"

14

◆ THE MAN FROM SNOWY RIVER ◆

There was movement at the station, for the word has passed around
That the colt from old Regret had got away,
And had joined the wild bush horses — he was worth a thousand pound,
So all the cracks had gathered to the fray.
All the tried and noted riders from the stations near and far
Had mustered at the homestead overnight,
For the bushmen love hard riding where the wild bush horses are,
And the stockhorse snuffs the battle with delight.

15

There was Harrison, who made his pile when Pardon won the cup,

The old man with his hair as white as snow;

But few could ride beside him when his blood was fairly up —

He would go wherever horse and man could go.

And Clancy of the Overflow came down to lend a hand,

No better horseman ever held the reins;

For never horse could throw him while the saddle girths would stand,

He learnt to ride while droving on the plains.

✤ T H E   M A N   F R O M   S N O W Y   R I V E R ✤

And one was there, a stripling on a small and weedy beast,
He was something like a racehorse undersized,
With a touch of Timor pony — three parts thoroughbred at least —
And such as are by mountain horsemen prized.
He was hard and tough and wiry — just the sort that won't say die —
There was courage in his quick impatient tread;
And he bore the badge of gameness in his bright and fiery eye,
And the proud and lofty carriage of his head.

But still so slight and weedy, one would doubt his power to stay,
And the old man said, "That horse will never do
For a long and tiring gallop — lad, you'd better stop away,
Those hills are far too rough for such as you."
So he waited sad and wistful — only Clancy stood his friend —
"I think we ought to let him come," he said;
"I warrant he'll be with us when he's wanted at the end,
For both his horse and he are mountain bred.

"He hails from Snowy River, up by Kosciusko's side,
Where the hills are twice as steep and twice as rough,
Where a horse's hoofs strike firelight from the flint stones every stride,
The man that holds his own is good enough.
And the Snowy River riders on the mountains make their home,
Where the river runs those giant hills between;
I have seen full many horsemen since I first commenced to roam,
But nowhere yet such horsemen have I seen."

So he went — they found the horses by the big mimosa clump —
They raced away towards the mountain's brow,
And the old man gave his orders, "Boys, go at them from the jump,
No use to try for fancy riding now.
And, Clancy, you must wheel them, try and wheel them to the right.
Ride boldly, lad, and never fear the spills,
For never yet was rider that could keep the mob in sight,
If once they gain the shelter of those hills."

So Clancy rode to wheel them — he was racing on the wing
Where the best and boldest riders take their place,
And he raced his stockhorse past them, and he made the ranges ring
With the stockwhip, as he met them face to face.
Then they halted for a moment, while he swung the dreaded lash,
But they saw their well-loved mountain full in view,
And they charged beneath the stockwhip with a sharp and sudden dash,
And off into the mountain scrub they flew.

✦ T H E M A N F R O M S N O W Y R I V E R ✦

Then fast the horsemen followed, where the gorges deep and black
Resounded to the thunder of their tread,
And the stockwhips woke the echoes, and they fiercely answered back
From cliffs and crags that beetled overhead.
And upward, ever upward, the wild horses held their way,
Where mountain ash and kurrajong grew wide;
And the old man muttered fiercely, "We may bid the mob good day,
No man can hold them down the other side."

When they reached the mountain's summit, even Clancy took a pull,
It well might make the boldest hold their breath,
The wild hop scrub grew thickly, and the hidden ground was full
Of wombat holes, and any slip was death.
But the man from Snowy River let the pony have his head,
And he swung his stockwhip round and gave a cheer,
And he raced him down the mountain like a torrent down its bed,
While the others stood and watched in very fear.

He sent the flint stones flying, but the pony kept his feet,
He cleared the fallen timber in his stride,
And the man from Snowy River never shifted in his seat —
It was grand to see that mountain horseman ride.
Through the stringybarks and saplings, on the rough and broken ground,
Down the hillside at a racing pace he went;
And he never drew the bridle till he landed safe and sound,
At the bottom of that terrible descent.

31

❖ S N O W Y   R I V E R   R I D E R S ❖

✦ T H E   M A N   F R O M   S N O W Y   R I V E R   ✦

He was right among the horses as they climbed the further hill,
And the watcher's on the mountain standing mute,
Saw him ply the stockwhip fiercely, he was right among them still,
As he raced across the clearing in pursuit.
Then they lost him for a moment, where two mountain gullies met
In the ranges, but a final glimpse reveals
On a dim and distant hillside the wild horses racing yet,
With the man from Snowy River at their heels.

✥ T H E   M A N   F R O M   S N O W Y   R I V E R   ✥

And he ran them single-handed till their sides were white with foam.
He followed like a bloodhound on their track,
Till they halted cowed and beaten, then he turned their heads for home,
And alone and unassisted brought them back.
But his hardy mountain pony he could scarcely raise a trot,
He was blood from hip to shoulder from the spur;
But his pluck was still undaunted, and his courage fiery hot,
For never yet was mountain horse a cur.

✦ T H E M A N F R O M S N O W Y R I V E R ✦

And down by Kosciusko, where the pine-clad ridges raise

Their torn and rugged battlements on high,

Where the air is clear as crystal, and the white stars fairly blaze

At midnight in the cold and frosty sky,

And where around The Overflow the reed beds sweep and sway

To the breezes, and the rolling plains are wide,

The man from Snowy River is a household word today,

And the stockmen tell the story of his ride.

◆ A MOUNTAIN STATION ◆

I bought a run a while ago,
　On country rough and ridgy,
Where wallaroos and wombats grow —
　The Upper Murrumbidgee.
The grass is rather scant, it's true,
　But this a fair exchange is,
The sheep can see a lovely view
　By climbing up the ranges.

And "She-oak Flat" 's the station's name,
　I'm not surprised at that, sirs:
The oaks were there before I came,
　And I supplied the flat, sirs.
A man would wonder how it's done.
　The stock so soon decreases —
They sometimes tumble off the run
　And break themselves to pieces.

I've tried to make expenses meet,
  But wasted all my labours,
The sheep the dingoes didn't eat
  Were stolen by the neighbours.
They stole my pears — my native pears —
  Those thrice-convicted felons,
And ravished from me unawares
  My crop of paddymelons.

And sometimes under sunny skies,
  Without an explanation,
The Murrumbidgee used to rise
  And overflow the station.
But this was caused (as now I know)
  When summer sunshine glowing
Had melted all Kiandra's snow
  And set the river going.

And in the news, perhaps you read:
"Stock passings. Puckawidgee,
Fat cattle: Seven hundred head
  Swept down the Murrumbidgee;
Their destination's quite obscure,
  But, somehow, there's a notion,
Unless the river falls, they're sure
  To reach the Southern Ocean."

So after that I'll give it best;
  No more with Fate I'll battle.
I'll let the river take the rest,
  For those were all my cattle.
And with one comprehensive curse
  I close my brief narration,
And advertise it in my verse —
  "For Sale! A Mountain Station".

◆ WITH THE CATTLE ◆

The drought is down on field and flock,
  The river bed is dry;
And we shift the starving stock
  Before the cattle die.
We muster up with weary hearts
  At breaking of the day,
And turn our heads to foreign parts,
  To take the stock away.
And it's hunt 'em up and dog 'em,
And it's get the whip and flog 'em,
For it's weary work is droving when they're dying every day;
By stock routes bare and eaten,
On dusty roads and beaten,
With half a chance to save their lives we take the stock away.

We cannot use the whip for shame
  On beasts that crawl along;
We have to drop the weak and lame,
  And try to save the strong;
The wrath of God is on the track,
  The drought fiend holds his sway,
With blows and cries and stockwhip crack
  We take the stock away.
As they fall we leave them lying,
With the crows to watch them dying,
Grim sextons of the Overland that fasten on their prey;
By the fiery dust storm drifting,
And the mocking mirage shifting,
In heat and drought and hopeless pain we take the stock away.

In dull despair the days go by
  With never hope of change,
But every stage we draw more nigh
  Towards the mountain range;
And some may live to climb the pass,
  And reach the great plateau,
And revel in the mountain grass,
  By streamlets fed with snow.
As the mountain wind is blowing
It starts the cattle lowing,
And calling to each other down the dusty long array;
And there speaks a grizzled drover;
"Well, thank God, the worst is over,
The creatures smell the mountain grass that's twenty miles away."

They press towards the mountain grass,
  They look with eager eyes
Along the rugged stony pass,
  That slopes towards the skies;
Their feet may bleed from rocks and stones,
  But though the blood-drop starts,
They struggle on with stifled groans,
  For hope is in their hearts.
And the cattle that are leading,
Though their feet are worn and bleeding,
Are breaking to a kind of run — pull up, and let them go!
For the mountain wind is blowing,
And the mountain grass is growing,
They settle down by running streams ice-cold with melted snow.

53

✤ WITH THE CATTLE ✤

The days are done of heat and drought
　Upon the stricken plain;
The wind has shifted right about,
　And brought the welcome rain;
The river runs with sullen roar,
　All flecked with yellow foam,
And we must take the road once more,
　To bring the cattle home.
And it's "Lads! we'll raise a chorus,
There's a pleasant trip before us."
And the horses bound beneath us as we start them down the track;
And the drovers canter, singing,
Through the sweet green grasses springing,
Towards the far-off mountain land, to bring the cattle back.

Are these the beasts we brought away
　That move so lively now?
They scatter off like flying spray
　Across the mountain's brow;
And dashing down the rugged range
　We hear the stockwhip crack,
Good faith, it is a welcome change
　To bring such cattle back.
And it's "Steady down the lead there!"
And it's "Let 'em stop and feed there!"
For they're wild as mountain eagles and their sides are all afoam;
But they're settling down already,
And they'll travel nice and steady,
With cheery call and jest and song we fetch the cattle home.

Robert Lovett

We have to watch them close at night
  For fear they'll make a rush,
And break away in headlong flight
  Across the open bush;
And by the campfire's cheery blaze,
  With mellow voice and strong,
We hear the lonely watchman raise
  The Overlander's song:
"Oh! it's when we're done with roving,
With the camping and the droving,
It's homeward down the Bland we'll go, and never more we'll roam;"
While the stars shine out above us,
Like the eyes of those who love us —
The eyes of those who watch and wait to greet the cattle home.

The plains are all awave with grass,
  The skies are deepest blue;
And leisurely the cattle pass
  And feed the long day through;
But when we sight the station gate,
  We make the stockwhips crack,
A welcome sound to those who wait
  To greet the cattle back:
And through the twilight falling
We hear their voices calling,
As the cattle splash across the ford and churn it into foam;
And the children run to meet us,
And our wives and sweethearts greet us,
Their heroes from the Overland who brought the cattle home.

56

57

◆ On Kiley's Run ◆

The roving breezes come and go
    On Kiley's Run,
The sleepy river murmurs low,
And far away one dimly sees
Beyond the stretch of forest trees —
Beyond the foothills dusk and dun —
The ranges sleeping in the sun
    On Kiley's Run.

'Tis many years since first I came
    To Kiley's Run,
More years than I would care to name
Since I, a stripling, used to ride
For miles and miles at Kiley's side,
The while in stirring tones he told
The stories of the days of old
    On Kiley's Run.

I see the old bush homestead now
    On Kiley's Run,
Just nestled down beneath the brow
Of one small ridge above the sweep
Of river flat, where willows weep
And jasmine flowers and roses bloom,
The air was laden with perfume
    On Kiley's Run.

We lived the good old station life
  On Kiley's Run,
With little thought of care or strife.
Old Kiley seldom used to roam,
He liked to make the Run his home,
The swagman never turned away
With empty hand at close of day
  From Kiley's Run.

We kept a racehorse now and then
  On Kiley's Run,
And neighb'ring stations brought their men
To meetings where the sport was free,
And dainty ladies came to see
Their champions ride; with laugh and song
The old house rang the whole night long
  On Kiley's Run.

The station hands were friends I wot
 On Kiley's Run,
A reckless, merry-hearted lot —
All splendid riders, and they knew
The "boss" was kindness through and through.
Old Kiley always stood their friend,
And so they served him to the end
 On Kiley's Run.

But droughts and losses came apace
 To Kiley's Run.
Till ruin stared him in the face;
He toiled and toiled while lived the light,
He dreamed of overdrafts at night:
At length, because he could not pay,
His bankers took the stock away
 From Kiley's Run.

Old Kiley stood and saw them go
  From Kiley's Run.
The well-bred cattle marching slow;
His stockmen, mates for many a day,
They wrung his hand and went away.
Too old to make another start,
Old Kiley died — of broken heart,
  On Kiley's Run.

The owner lives in England now
  Of Kiley's Run.
He knows a racehorse from a cow;
But that is all he knows of stock:
His chiefest care is how to dock
Expenses, and he sends from town
To cut the shearers' wages down
  On Kiley's Run.

There are no neighbours anywhere
  Near Kiley's Run.
The hospitable homes are bare,
The gardens gone; for no pretence
Must hinder cutting down expense:
The homestead that we held so dear
Contains a half-paid overseer
  On Kiley's Run.

All life and sport and hope have died
  On Kiley's Run.
No longer there the stockmen ride;
For sour-faced boundary riders creep
On mongrel horses after sheep,
Through ranges where, at racing speed,
Old Kiley used to "wheel the lead"
  On Kiley's Run.

There runs a lane for thirty miles
  Through Kiley's Run.
On either side the herbage smiles,
But wretched trav'lling sheep must pass
Without a drink or blade of grass
Thro' that long lane of death and shame:
The weary drovers curse the name
  On Kiley's Run.

The name itself is changed of late
  Of Kiley's Run.
They call it "Chandos Park Estate".
The lonely swagman through the dark
Must hump his swag past Chandos Park.
The name is English, don't you see,
The old name sweeter sounds to me
  Of "Kiley's Run".

I cannot guess what fate will bring
  To Kiley's Run —
For chances come and changes ring —
I scarcely think 'twill always be
Locked up to suit an absentee;
And if he lets it out in farms
His tenants soon will carry arms
  On Kiley's Run.

◆ BRUMBY'S RUN ◆

It lies beyond the western pines
  Towards the sinking sun,
And not a survey mark defines
  The bounds of "Brumby's run".

On odds and ends of mountain land
  On tracks of range and rock,
Where no one else can make a stand,
  Old Brumby rears his stock —

✦ S N O W Y   R I V E R   R I D E R S ✦

BRUMBY'S RUN

A wild, unhandled lot they are
  Of every shape and breed,
They venture out 'neath moon and star
  Along the flats to feed.

✢ B R U M B Y ' S   R U N ✢

But when the dawn makes pink the sky
  And steals along the plain,
The Brumby horses turn and fly
  Towards the hills again.

The traveller by the mountain track
  May hear their hoofbeats pass,
And catch a glimpse of brown and black,
  Dim shadows on the grass.

❖ B R U M B Y ' S   R U N ❖

✦ S N O W Y   R I V E R   R I D E R S ✦

✦ Brumby's Run ✦

The eager stock horse pricks his ears
   And lifts his head on high
In wild excitement when he hears
   The Brumby mob go by.

Old Brumby asks no price or fee
   O'er all his wide domains:
The man who yards his stock is free
   To keep them for his pains.

✦ B R U M B Y ' S   R U N ✦

So, off to scour the mountainside
  With eager eyes aglow,
To strongholds where the wild mobs hide
  The gully-rakers go.

A rush of horses through the trees,
  A red shirt making play;
A sound of stockwhips on the breeze,
  They vanish far away!

Ah, me! before our day is done
    We long with bitter pain
To ride once more on Brumby's run
    And yard his mob again.

✦ SNOWY RIVER RIDERS ✦